You Give
Great Meeting, Sid

Doonesbury books by G. B. Trudeau

a Doonesbury book by

G B Trudeau.

You Give
Great Meeting, Sid

An Owl Book **Holt, Rinehart and Winston / New York**

Published by Holt, Rinehart and Winston,
383 Madison Avenue, New York, New York 10017.

Published simultaneously in Canada by Holt, Rinehart and
Winston of Canada, Limited.

Library of Congress Catalog Card Number: 83-80662

ISBN: 0-03-061733-2

First Edition

Printed in the United States of America

The cartoons in this book have appeared in newspapers
in the United States and abroad under the auspices of
Universal Press Syndicate.

1 3 5 7 9 10 8 6 4 2

ISBN 0-03-061733-2

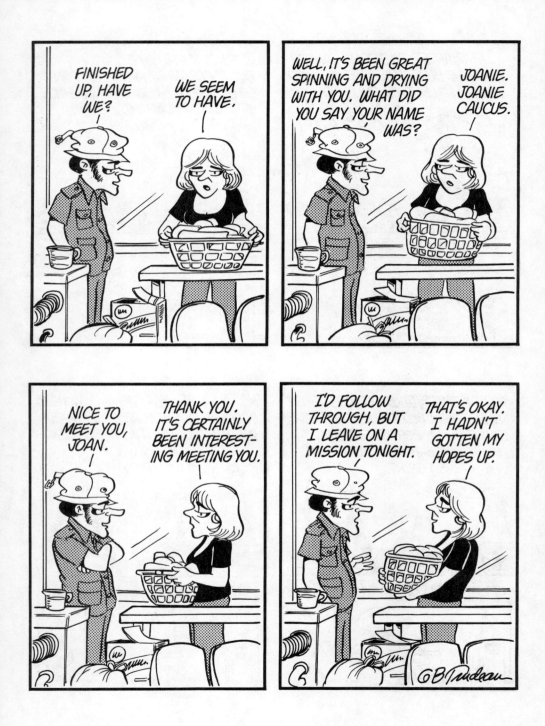

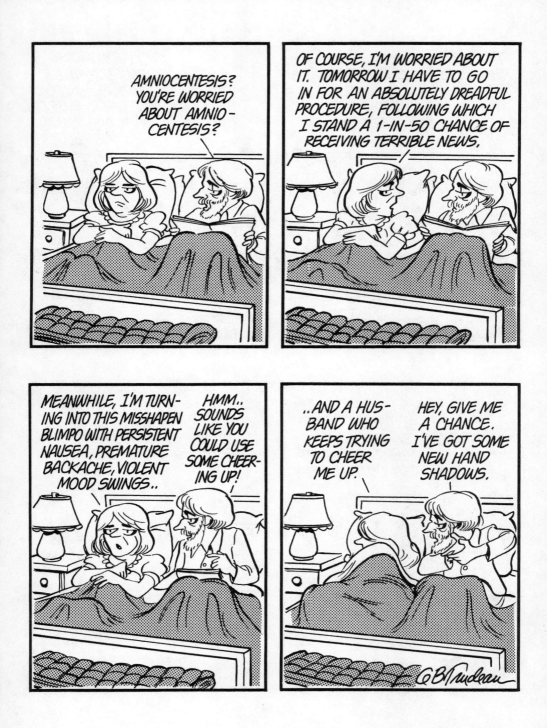

WHERE YOU HEADED, OLD BOY?
WEST BEIRUT, OF COURSE! WHERE THE ACTION IS! I APPRECIATE THE LIFT.
YOU'RE LUCKY I CAME ALONG. TAXI FARE TO WEST BEI-RUT CAN RUN AS MUCH AS $200.
NO PROBLEM. I'M HERE ON AN EXPENSE ACCOUNT.
YOU'LL NEED IT. I TAKE IT YOU'RE NEW TO WAR ZONE REPORTING.
NOT AT ALL. WHAT MAKES YOU SAY THAT?
YOUR CLOTHES. THEY LOOK CLEAN, FRESH. FREE OF STATIC CLING.
I CAN EXPLAIN THAT.
©B Trudeau

WHAT IS IT, SERGEANT?
THE PRELIMINARY COUNT OF TERRORIST EVACUEES HAS ARRIVED, SIR.
AT LAST! LET'S SEE.
WAIT A MINUTE! THIS IS IT? THIS IS THE OFFICIAL P.L.O. COUNT?
YES, SIR.
THERE ARE ONLY **FIVE** TERRORISTS IN BEIRUT?
I GUESS WE GOT MORE OF THEM THAN WE THOUGHT, SIR.
©B Trudeau

I WILL TELL YOU QUITE FRANKLY, MR. HEDLEY. I AM ASHAMED OF NOTHING WE HAVE DONE IN THIS COUNTRY. THE ARMY HAS BEHAVED WITH **GREAT** RESTRAINT.
COME NOW, CAPTAIN, SURELY YOU WILL CONCEDE THAT..
EXCUSE ME A MOMENT, WILL YOU PLEASE, MR. HEDLEY..
OKAY, PRIVATE, PICK UP THAT CIGARETTE BUTT! YOU KNOW MY ORDERS AGAINST LITTERING IN LEBANON!
SORRY, SIR.
WE'RE **GUESTS** IN THIS COUNTRY, SOLDIER!
GB Trudeau

..AND WE FEEL WE'VE BEEN MORE THAN FLEXIBLE DURING THE NEGOTIATIONS. THE DROPPING OF OUR DEMAND FOR A LIST OF P.L.O. EVACUEES IS A GOOD EXAMPLE.
BUT WHY DID YOU NEED SUCH A LIST IN THE FIRST PLACE?
TO MONITOR COMPLIANCE, OF COURSE. TO MAKE SURE ALL THE TERRORISTS LEFT.
BUT ONCE YOU HAD ALL THEIR NAMES AND ADDRESSES IN YOUR COMPUTER, COULDN'T THAT HAVE LED TO ALL KINDS OF ABUSE?
ABUSE? LIKE WHAT?
WELL, LIKE, WHAT WOULD'VE KEPT YOU FROM SENDING THE GUERRILLAS A LOT OF JUNK MAIL?
WE WERE PREPARED TO OFFER CERTAIN GUARANTEES.
G.B. Trudeau

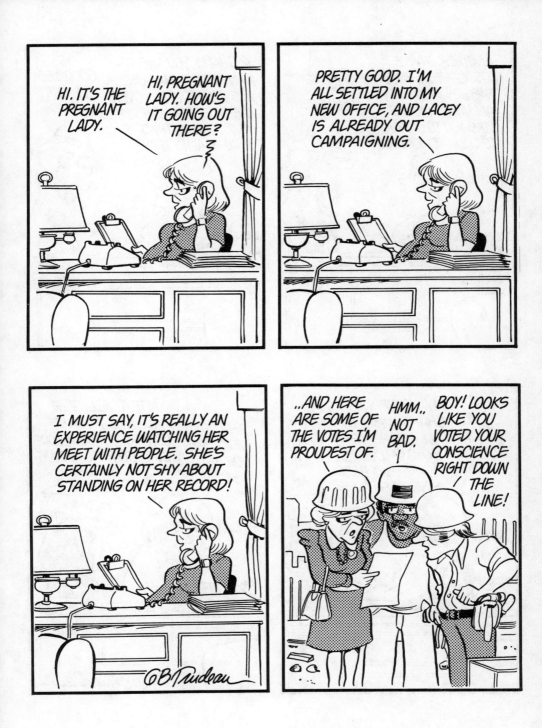

NAME?
HARRIS, ZONKER.
WHICH COMPANIES ARE YOU INTERESTED IN INTERVIEWING WITH?
DEPENDS. WHAT HAVE YOU GOT?
MR. HARRIS, THERE ARE OVER 200 COMPANIES RECRUITING ON CAMPUS. WHAT ARE YOUR GENERAL AREAS OF INTEREST?
AERODYNAMICS. DESIGNER JEANS. ROOFING SUPPLIES. THAT SORT OF THING.
WHAT SORT OF THING?
YOU KNOW, LIQUIDITY. POINT-OF-SALE. MARGIN ACCOUNTS. FAST LANE.
CAREFUL, ZONK. YOU'LL PEAK BEFORE THE INTERVIEWS.
GBTrudeau

EVERY NOW AND THEN, WE ON "LATE NIGHT" LIKE TO INVITE A BUSINESS TYCOON ON THE SHOW, AND SO WE DO. RIGHT, PAUL?
YOU'RE A FRESH KICK, DAVE! YOU KILL ME!
THANKS, PAUL. WITH US HERE TONIGHT IS MOGUL-IN-THE-NEWS PHIL SLACKMEYER. PHIL, WHAT'S THE STORY ON THIS BIG MERGER WITH TRENDEX?
IT'S NOT A MERGER, MR. LETTERMAN. IT'S CORPORATE WAR.
AHA. SO WE'RE TALKING ABOUT AN UNFRIENDLY TAKEOVER HERE, I'M GUESSING. NOW, WHAT'LL YOU DO TO TRENDEX IF YOU GET IT?
ROUGHLY WHAT ROME DID TO CARTHAGE. WE'LL ABSORB THEIR OPERATIONS AND RAZE THEIR CORPORATE STRUCTURE! TRENDEX WILL CEASE TO EXIST!
AMAZING. SAY, COULD WE GET A TIGHT SHOT OF THE VEINS ON PHIL'S NECK HERE?
WOMEN AND CHILDREN WILL BE PROVIDED FOR, OF COURSE..
©B Trudeau

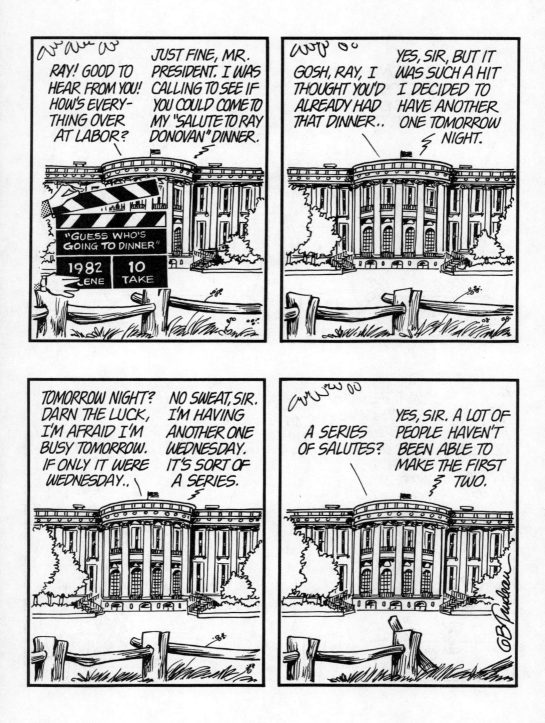

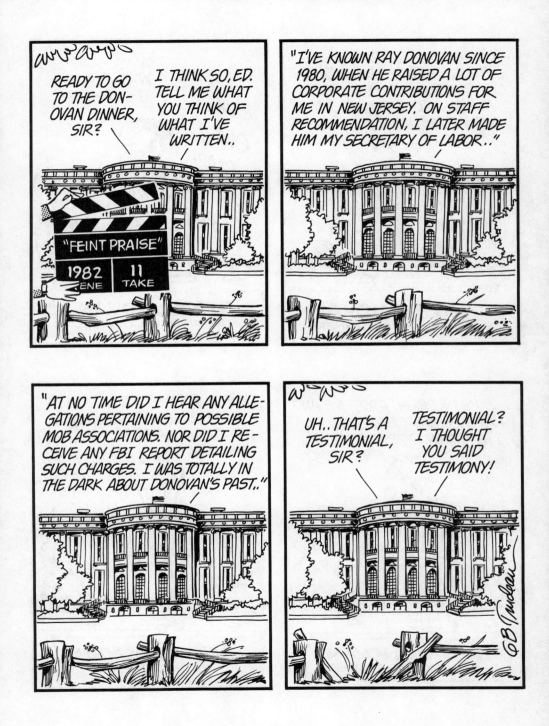

HI, SAILOR! WELCOME TO THE NEIGHBORHOOD. THE NAME'S ALICE P. SCHWARTZMAN! WHO ARE YOU?
UH.. DUKE. THE NAME'S DUKE.
PLEASED TO MEET YOU, DUCK. WANT PART OF MY PAPER? IT'S ONLY THREE WEEKS OLD!
Saks
YEAH.. YOU GOT THE SPORTS SECTION?
SURE. YOU FOLLOW THE PONIES?
NAH. I JUST PUT MY LAST TEN BUCKS ON THE BREWERS.
THIS AIN'T YOUR DAY, DUCKS.
© B Trudeau

OKAY, WHAT WE'RE GOING TO DO NOW IS LISTEN TO A TAPE OF A NORMAL CHILDBIRTH. THE SOUNDS SHOULD HELP YOU PICTURE YOURSELVES IN THE DELIVERY ROOM.
AANH! AANH! PUFF!
THE MOTHER HAS GONE INTO HER FINAL CONTRACTIONS AND IS BEARING DOWN!
DEEP BREATH! BEAR DOWN! HERE IT COMES!
THAT'S THE MONITRICE COACHING THE MOTHER.
MY GOD! HIS HEAD LOOKS LIKE A MELON!
THAT'S THE FATHER.
GB Trudeau

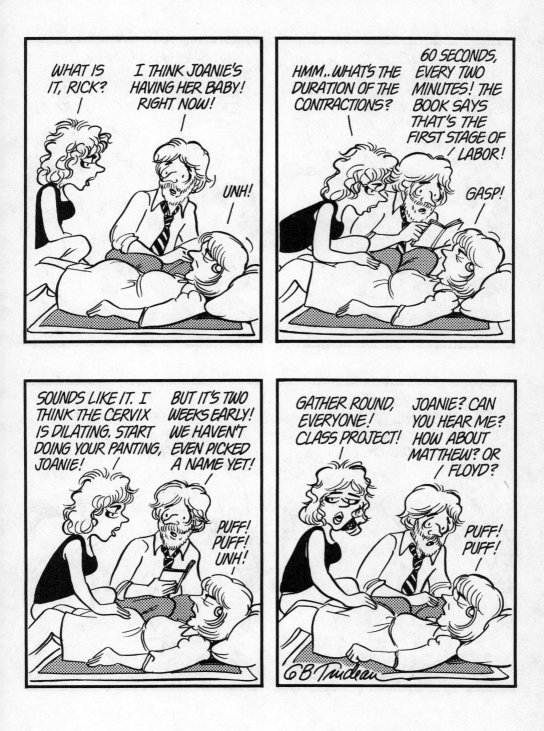